Working Animals

Crime-Fighting Animals

by Julie Murray

Dash!

2

LEVELED READERS

An Imprint of Abdo Zoom • abdobooks.com

Dash!
LEVELED READERS

Level 1 – Beginning
Short and simple sentences with familiar words or patterns for children who are beginning to understand how letters and sounds go together.

Level 2 – Emerging
Longer words and sentences with more complex language patterns for readers who are practicing common words and letter sounds.

Level 3 – Transitional
More developed language and vocabulary for readers who are becoming more independent.

THIS BOOK CONTAINS RECYCLED MATERIALS

abdobooks.com

Published by Abdo Zoom, a division of ABDO, PO Box 398166, Minneapolis, Minnesota 55439. Copyright © 2020 by Abdo Consulting Group, Inc. International copyrights reserved in all countries. No part of this book may be reproduced in any form without written permission from the publisher. Dash!™ is a trademark and logo of Abdo Zoom.

Printed in the United States of America, North Mankato, Minnesota.
052019
092019

Photo Credits: Alamy, iStock, Shutterstock
Production Contributors: Kenny Abdo, Jennie Forsberg, Grace Hansen, John Hansen
Design Contributors: Dorothy Toth, Neil Klinepier

Library of Congress Control Number: 2018963325

Publisher's Cataloging in Publication Data

Names: Murray, Julie, author.
Title: Crime-fighting animals / by Julie Murray.
Description: Minneapolis, Minnesota : Abdo Zoom, 2020 | Series: Working animals | Includes online resources and index.
Identifiers: ISBN 9781532127311 (lib. bdg.) | ISBN 9781532128295 (ebook) | ISBN 9781532128783 (Read-to-me ebook)
Subjects: LCSH: Working animals--Juvenile literature. | Animals in police work--Juvenile literature. | Police dogs--Juvenile literature. | Police horses--Juvenile literature.
Classification: DDC 363.2--dc23

Table of Contents

Crime-Fighting Animals

SHERIFF

Sarge is a German shepherd. He is working. His job is to fight crime!

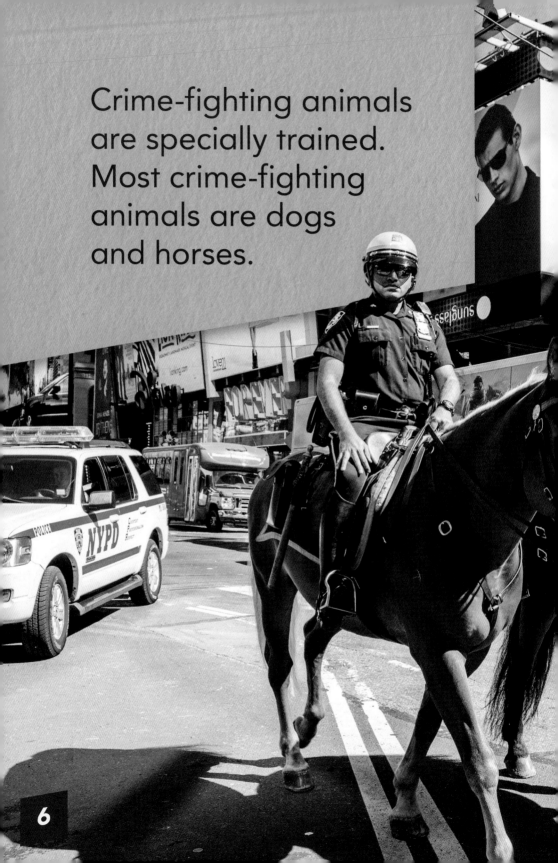

Crime-fighting animals are specially trained. Most crime-fighting animals are dogs and horses.

Dogs go to K-9 School for training for 12 weeks. They work with their **handlers**.

Dogs and handlers have a close **bond**.

Police dogs are smart, strong, and fast. They listen to **commands**.

Many crime-fighting animals wear special **gear**. Some dogs wear bulletproof vests. This keeps them safe.

What They Do

Some dogs work at airports. They are often seen sniffing luggage. They are searching for illegal drugs and weapons.

Tracking dogs help find missing people or items. They also help find **suspects** that are hiding.

Bloodhounds make good tracking dogs.

Some police officers ride horses. They are able to help control a crowd. They often work at concerts or parades. Many wear eye-shields and leg protectors.

Crime-fighting animals
work to keep people safe.
They make the world a
better place.

More Facts

- Dogs have an incredible sense of smell. Their sense of smell is likely around 100,000 times greater than ours.

- K-9 is short for "canine." "Canine" comes from the Latin word *caninus* meaning "of the dog."

- Most K-9 dogs only work for about six years.

Glossary

bond – a feeling that brings people and animals together.

command – to lead and control.

gear – any equipment, clothes, or tools used for a particular purpose.

handler – a person who trains and has charge of an animal.

suspect – one who is suspected of committing a crime.

Index

Online Resources

Booklinks
NONFICTION NETWORK
FREE! ONLINE NONFICTION RESOURCES

To learn more about crime-fighting animals, please visit **abdobooklinks.com** or scan this QR code. These links are routinely monitored and updated to provide the most current information available.